around the oval

Violeta Ivanova

BookLeaf Publishing

India | USA | UK

Presentation by *BookLeaf Publishing*

Web: www.bookleafpub.com

E-mail: info@bookleafpub.com

ISBN: 9789357446341

First edition 2022

DEDICATION

to all the people who were there to tell me 'hEaLinG iSn't liNEar',

I love you, have this: 0

cult kin

silly little child how far you have come and
strayed
they never stay, not even the ones who are
blood-bound
your bloodhound can bite heads off but can you
arrange yours, to play with.
pretty petty if you ask me but you never do
you don't like being told who to trust to quiet
your mind
they're not marbles you know

the gravity of the mistakes you make is defined
by the reasoning behind the choice to make
them, pain is what you make it. familiarity is a
weapon, so why do you get so close and lie
lie that you won't hurt, them, anyone you'd
never

who   hurt me, am I right

iodine cap

shake shake it stole your autonomy
the lull of the bottle of pills sings you to sleep
and jolts you aware within seconds, your skin is
grey and your face is missing
you are free to forget me but remember where it
rolled behind the cabinet with the mirror in
which you smile
your smile, too wide for reality, your eyes took a
screenshot that you did not develop correctly,
this artificial light hot flashes, hot bodies and
cold sweat pooling on your temples you're not
supposed to mix that with your prescription
you'll see god and then what? gain
consciousness and a second mind your meds and
your mind will mend the holes you bore in cold
sweat, low highs and that artificial lightlife life
artifice art are a r re yo u   okay

this is insanitary go pick it up right now

lilac bricks

my nails turn and my mouth bleeds to build the home inside of me.

I am an island barren and deserted, swallowed by years of waves, coming in, never out, gentle destruction masked as divine retribution, my karma and my cosmos. where is the consent in leaving the sand to skin you.   why do this?
I can save us or fold, home is not a place, it's not a person, it's not a promise, it's a fear.

acetone

the distance between the door and the rest of the
world is two sips of nail polish remover and an
arm scraping the popcorn off, really? the
distance between reality and that fever-dream
like plan was 1.5 and you had it, one can only
assume.

you wonder if it did anything for you,

I guess we'll never know

Mors

what are the things we over explain and who
gets to play the role of god, to brand the cattle,
make amends, matters of mortality, what matters
if
the murderer, the victim, and the judge all in one
person, in a single cell reverberating church
bells; righteousness, vulgar yet pure, reverent
violence.

dash yourself dead against the bars, if, upside
down is the right side up, it's on my heart I made
sure to scar it there. a leash is still a leash no
matter the length, no need to overextend

hysteria

you have to be joking, these are just growing
pains
painted pain and blood in the paint, paint the
walls
with emotional excess, the exalt of the motion,
ignited
I started this, like sculpting, painting, poetry,
photography, sex love, alcohol, and got bored
and dropped it like it meant nothing.
I molt each time, forever mending and molding
an imperfect imbalanced shape, an abnormality,
chronic and not-so-uncommon but what do I
know if not myself

I dream of the day I wake up correct and
complete.
until then, we wake up, eat this pollution, drink
gasoline, abort our children, and paint the walls
with the pain others inflict and our own
growing pains

venom

I've known all this time and I chose to be better. speak then, inject it, tongues have twisted better minds than yours into submission, how dare you think you're any different. we are the same kind of putrid and unkind. there is a button for everyone and if there is only one button for all, one can only dream. I'm tired, inject it.

shallow mirrors

how much of this will you understand, most
chichés, only half the cringe, low blows served
on a backhanded lash   out
in this see-through house, we blow bubbles full
of poison at each other
but I will die on this hill, in the hole under that
tree, I will never stop looking for it.

there is a right and a wrong angle, take care or
you'll break
skin, they whisper, never forget they lie

porcelain teeth

at a glance you seem like you could have taught
me how to destroy people at chess. you look at
my life a while longer and realise I play people a
different way. we all crave structure but my
heritage costs more than my mind apparently.
you've changed because I gave you no choice.
I will not be carrying this blood forward, it dies
in my mind. It's five days from now and I feel
okay, what a concept. the train was stained and
falling apart. you'd say back in the day things
were simpler and I'd say of course,

your trains weren't falling apart.

setraline

let's find a way to make this sad. you had been falling for months, puking bile, trying to hold onto a warm gasp from lungs that do not belong to you. bodies can keep you warm for hours after the after-party, mind living in a haze? there's a pill for that, there's a dirty rag for every spill, bleach the floors, beach your dreams, drown who you are in dust at dusk on wet grass, dripping saliva high, who came for you, who comes for you, forget, forget, forget, forget, forget, and no matter how sloppy you really can't regret what is now just a hole in your memory.

I'm horny and I like em and I don't want you to come, ugh

why do you keep killing them

stop it get some help, change the code, go to
hell, you are your worst nightmare, reimagined,
the game replayed remastered. a jack in a deck
out on a pier, our pier
moldy emotional attachment, you slip and then
you have to crawl because what other choice
were you given. you use their heads as support,
eye sockets like bowling ball holes, you roll
never to score, never to be even, these are the
games we play
to win
to breathe

what a loser

UV

you want to talk about becomings, in this
tragedy of self, who comes out from behind the
curtain, what monsters do you feed
grind your pearls all you want, when this
happens you are in a clutch
it is absolutely your fault

what are we talking about what are we talking
about but the other way around
consumer pain, the squeeze of this costume, the
discomfort of your skin, clinging, clinical,
stitches that stay inside your body,
outperformed, overstayed their welcome, cry
and bleed, bleed and cry, talk to faces, eat hot
air, shower, drink water, go out to eat more hot
air and drink more than water, cry some more,
learn, repeat, bleed and cry, die a little inside,
you have to burn to be reborn

I told you

If I could bite my ears off I would, you spit in each other's mouths with such precision, I wonder if you've been doing it all your lives, self carelessness, I slip, my hands are calloused but at least I still have a grip on reality, do you know where you are and where you'll be in a year when it matters? affirmative action, I repeat myself because it's important and you keep chewing cartilage because it's easier. what a lame gimmick.

5 by 5 tangle

the wrong side is facing you, it broke you like fine lace against gravel and skin is supposed to build up thick death when bruised but yours became thinner. he wanted you to know how to sew and now you have needles in your arms, knots in your life, lost the beginning and only have the end tied to a fingertip. skip it, people tie red strings on their arms to remember, how much red did you carve to forget.

dstress

I was relieved to not wake up in agony as expected. I tell you almost everything and you try your best to understand. I wish I could give you more of me. I scratched the sky's skin and now I'm here, a body a body of water away and we've never been closer and that says a lot. you accomplish both and we equalise. I wish I didn't remind you of him.

split

they are shooting at you again, is this something
worth the discussion, cast in the void then cast
that away, storage is motherfucking expensive
empty boxes, empty words, empty touches, cold
fingers, cold sores, your body is sore and the
sugar in me is melting, I am not who I will be 18
minutes from now, I promise
it's ridiculous I remember this song, this love,
this hate,
less poetry but there's definitely pain in it
the sun is cold now and I move like a ghost

where you come from

dying in a small town grave, slipping sand that turns into tear shards tearing through the night you were left alone in that house you can find only creatures that lie. how many
sacrifices is your soul made out of? creatures that lie do not forget, bone knives and sharp corners of winding rooms that lead to drains in this reality. how it has shifted, how creatures lie to keep your mind in purgatory
you left the house and roamed the world, caffeine-induced anxiety, dewed grass, warm wind, and lights flickering as you trip on your untied shoelaces walking to another almost empty house, almost but just enough
to die in an old town grave, but bigger and shinier. you won't forget but you will be forgotten and your soul will return to you unearthing the lies laid where creatures sleep
we sleep on bones we kill with mouths full of flies full of lies

my, my

my intestines are on hooks above me, velvet
curtains of flesh, this isn't horror, real narcissism
and the idea of exposure so bright it melts your
face off, true vulnerability in the face of baseless
criticism, take your best shot I can break my
ribcage and make wings,
how are you going to reach me from your
pedestal, this play, you mannequin, with
microcuts in your eyes, you have already missed
because of your hypocrisy, I'll spare you your
plastic brain
I designed myself, I can do it again.

twin

the bright white knuckles on the smallest fist
you have ever seen would have, really should
have served as a reminder that you are not alone
in this. she finds this amusing, I suffer and she
finds this amusing. where I end she tries to
extend, you'd wonder who's taking care of
whom and is she meant to be here when I'm me.
demons children, they're all the same, we give
them names they stay, and leech a body force
out of itself,
long tongues splitting smiles for fun, for the
comedy for fuck's sake.
I have not been alone for a second of my life and
she plans on keeping it that way.

Canto XIII

I'm not going to. we gain the capacity to intellectualize our feelings to the point a professional appears to be a waste of time and money. we go to funerals that cost time and money, too much of either to ever go. those trees are now backrests, solace and sunshine, hot tea with the right kind of berries, pancakes with cream, a first kiss and your favourite rose bush blooming. hope there will come a day you wish to know more. and take the splinter out.

soup

one of these does not belong here and you cannot unsee it. I cannot unhear what has been said and what a shame. what a real shame.
it was cold in that room and now I'm ill, so I'm eating soup. this is how we get from point A to point B.